ORIGAMI
sea creatures

John Montroll

DOVER PUBLICATIONS, INC.
Mineola, New York

Bibliographical Note

This Dover edition, first published in 2004, is a new selections of designs from *Origami for the Enthusiast* (1979) and *Animal Origami for the Enthusiast* (1985) by John Montroll, both previously published by Dover Publications, Inc.

International Standard Book Number: 0-486-43971-2

Manufactured in the United States of America
Dover Publications, Inc., 31 East 2nd Street, Mineola, N.Y. 11501

INTRODUCTION

Origami is a challenging and unusual art. It requires square sheets of paper, which are formed into sculptures of animals or other objects by the process of folding.

Origami can be folded from almost any paper, but is most attractive when made from special paper called origami paper. Origami paper is square and usually comes in packets of assorted sizes and colors. It may be found in many variety and hobby stores. Difficult projects are easier to fold if you use the larger sizes of paper. The back side of each sheet of origami paper is white. In this book the colored side of the paper is indicated by the shaded areas.

It is important that you follow the directions carefully. The standard folds, from which the animals are created, are explained in detail at the beginning of the book. I have used the Randlett-Yoshizawa method of notation to indicate the folds.

The following rules should help guide you through the metamorphosis of folding. Examine step one; if there are any creased-folds in the square, fold them first. Make all further folds according to the instructions provided by lines, arrows and captions. Be aware of the instructions in the next step so that you know what each fold will become. Fold slowly and accurately and crease each fold with your fingernail to keep the folds crisp.

CONTENTS

Symbols

Lines

— — — — — — — — —   Valley fold, fold in front.

—··—··—··—··—··—   Mountain fold, fold behind.

————————————   Crease line.

···   X-ray or guide line.

Arrows

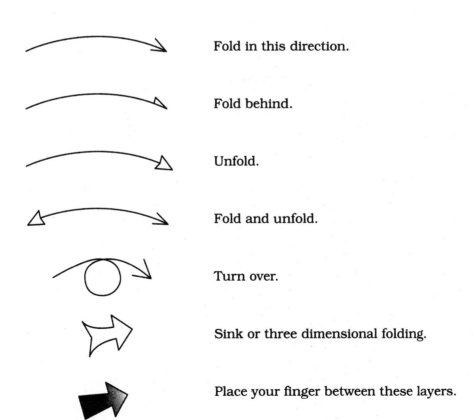

Fold in this direction.

Fold behind.

Unfold.

Fold and unfold.

Turn over.

Sink or three dimensional folding.

Place your finger between these layers.

Basic Folds

Rabbit Ear.

To fold a rabbit ear, one corner is folded in half and laid down to a side.

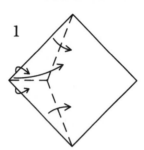

1

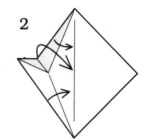

2

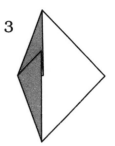

3

Fold a rabbit ear.

A three-dimensional intermediate step.

Double Rabbit Ear.

If you were to bend a straw you would be folding the double rabbit ear.

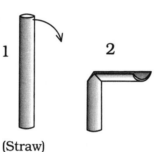

1

2

(Straw)

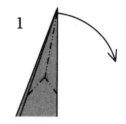

1

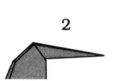

2

Make a double rabbit ear.

Squash Fold.

In a squash fold, some paper is opened and then made flat. The shaded arrow shows where to place your finger.

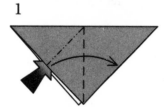

1

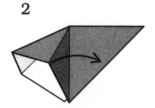

2

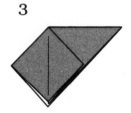

3

Squash-fold.

A three-dimensional intermediate step.

Petal Fold.

In a petal fold, one point is folded up while two opposite sides meet each other.

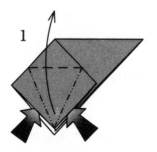

1

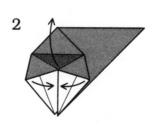

2

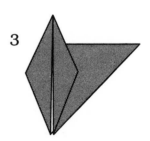

3

Petal-fold.

A three-dimensional intermediate step.

Inside Reverse Fold.

In an inside reverse fold, some paper is folded between layers. Here are two examples.

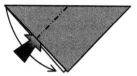 

Reverse-fold.

Reverse-fold.

Outside Reverse Fold.

Much of the paper must be unfolded to make an outside reverse fold.

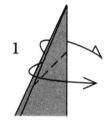 

Outside-reverse-fold.

Crimp Fold.

A crimp fold is a combination of two reverse folds.

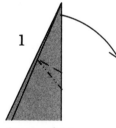 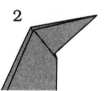

Crimp-fold.

Sink Fold.

In a sink fold, some of the paper without edges is folded inside. To do this fold, much of the model must be unfolded.

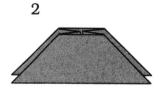

Sink.

Spread Squash Fold.

A cross between a squash fold and sink fold, some paper in the center is spread apart and then made flat.

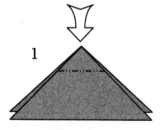 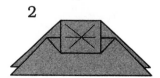 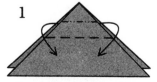

Spread-squash-fold.

Preliminary-fold

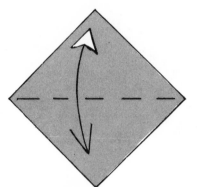

1. Fold diagonally in half, then unfold.

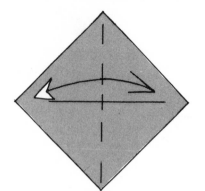

2. Repeat.

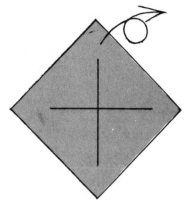

3. Turn over model, then turn clockwise.

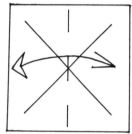

4. Fold in half, then unfold.

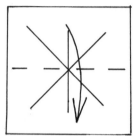

5. Fold in half.

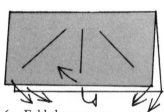

6a. Fold along creases.

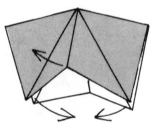

6b. Appearance just before completion.

Synopsis of steps 1-6b.

7. **PRELIMINARY-FOLD**

Bird Base

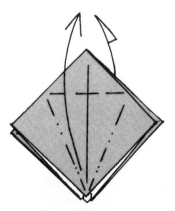

1. Begin with preliminary-fold, then petal-fold both sides.

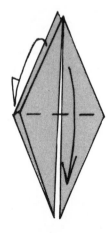

2. Fold tops of both sides down.

3. **BIRD BASE**

Brontosaurus Base

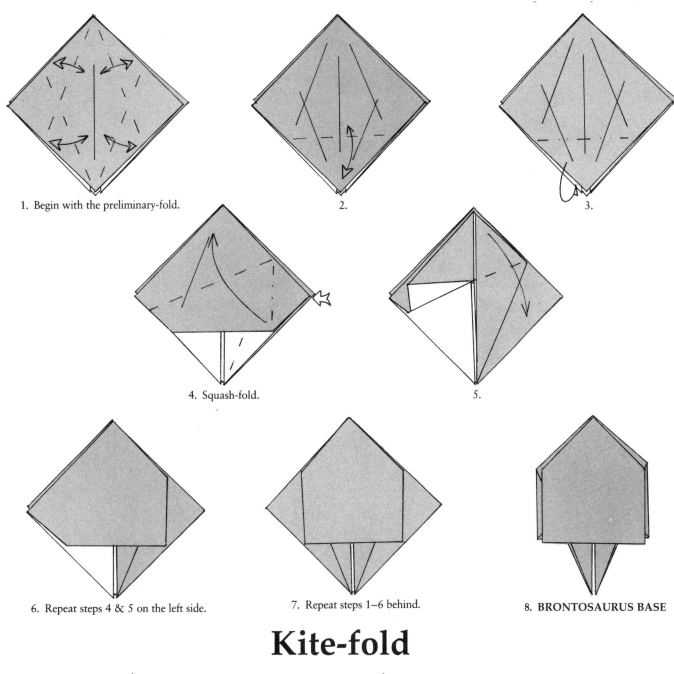

1. Begin with the preliminary-fold.

2.

3.

4. Squash-fold.

5.

6. Repeat steps 4 & 5 on the left side.

7. Repeat steps 1–6 behind.

8. **BRONTOSAURUS BASE**

Kite-fold

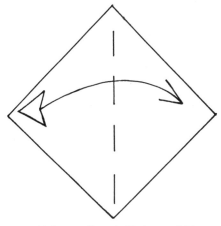

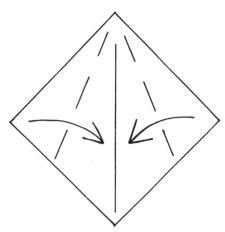

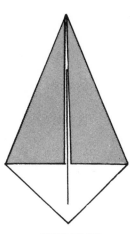

1. Fold diagonally in half, then unfold.

2. Valley-fold along lines to center crease.

3. **KITE-FOLD**

Wing-fold

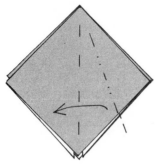 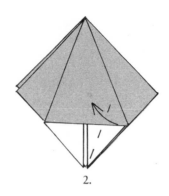  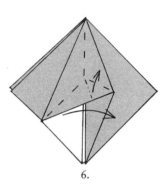

1. Begin with the preliminary-fold. Squash-fold.

2.

3.

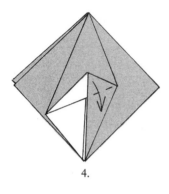 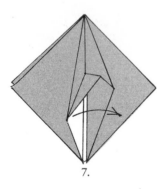 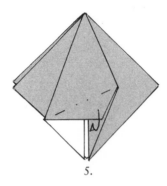 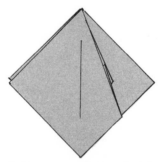 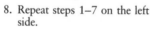 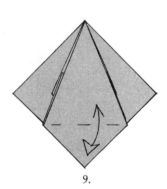

4.

5.

6.

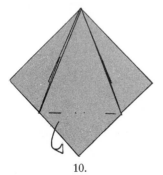 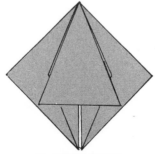

7.

8. Repeat steps 1–7 on the left side.

9.

10.

11. **WING-FOLD**

Fish

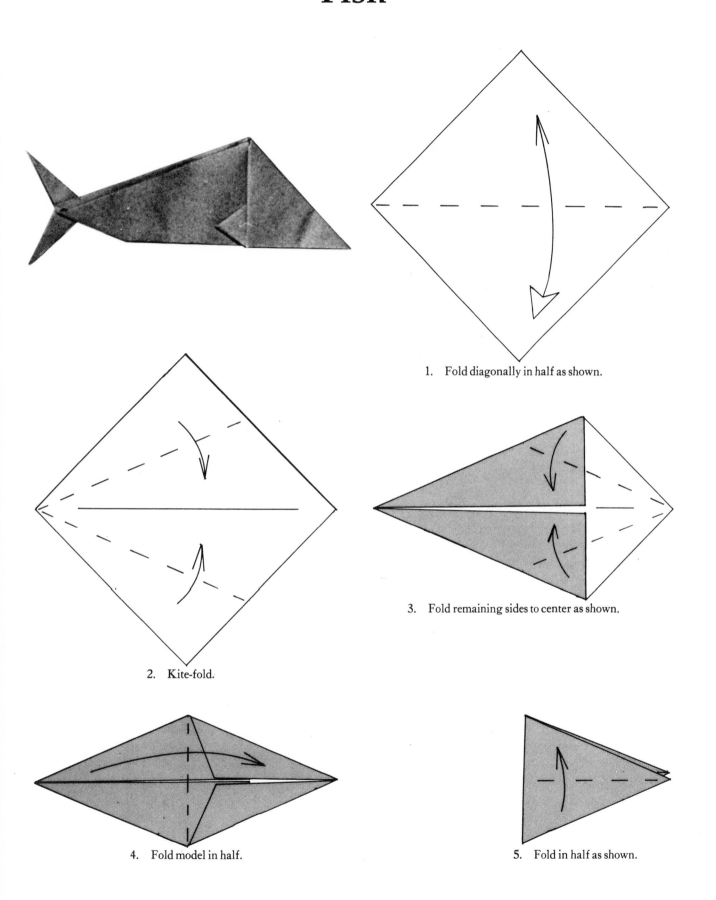

1. Fold diagonally in half as shown.

2. Kite-fold.

3. Fold remaining sides to center as shown.

4. Fold model in half.

5. Fold in half as shown.

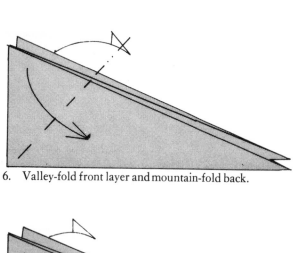
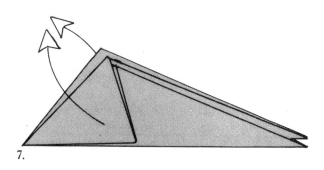

6. Valley-fold front layer and mountain-fold back.

7.

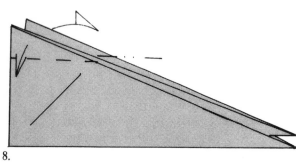

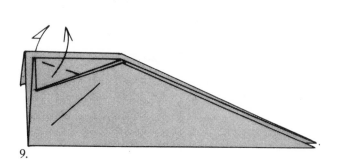

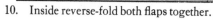

8.

9.

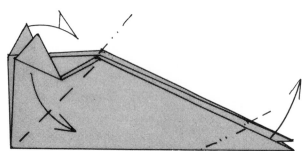

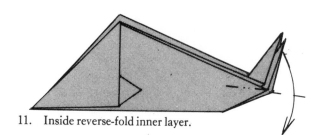

10. Inside reverse-fold both flaps together.

11. Inside reverse-fold inner layer.

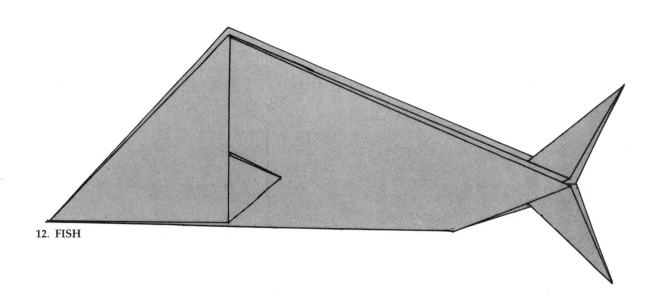

12. FISH

Goldfish

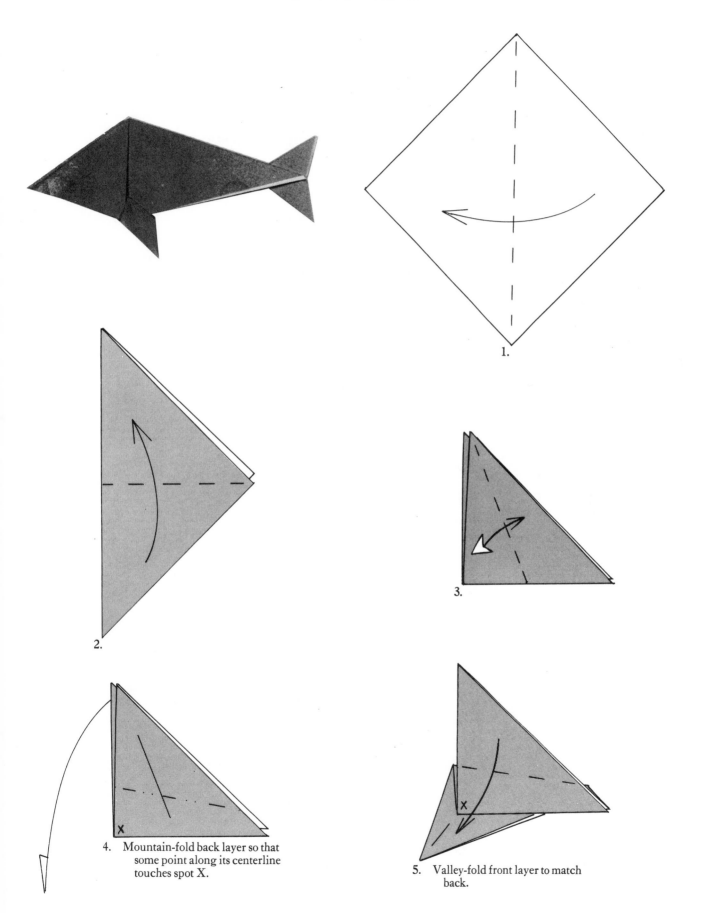

4. Mountain-fold back layer so that some point along its centerline touches spot X.

5. Valley-fold front layer to match back.

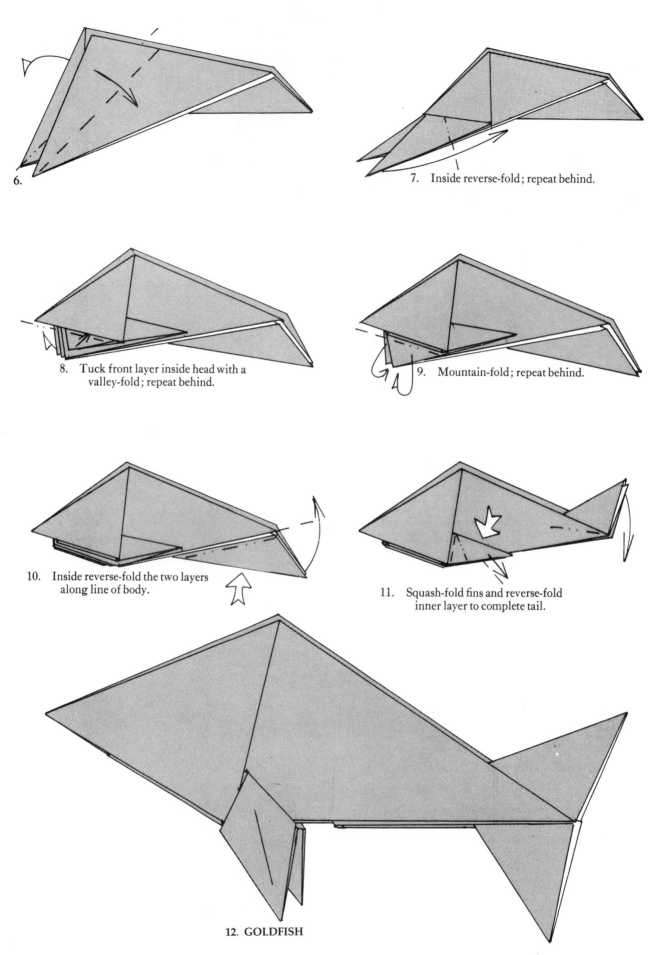

6.

7. Inside reverse-fold; repeat behind.

8. Tuck front layer inside head with a valley-fold; repeat behind.

9. Mountain-fold; repeat behind.

10. Inside reverse-fold the two layers along line of body.

11. Squash-fold fins and reverse-fold inner layer to complete tail.

12. GOLDFISH

Angelfish

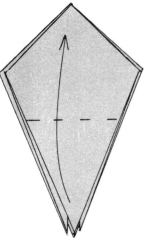

1. Begin with the bird base.

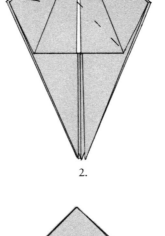

2.

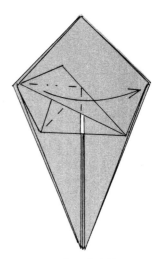

3. Squash-fold.

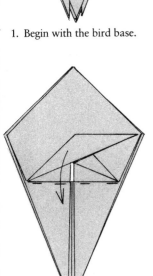

4.

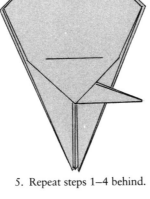

5. Repeat steps 1–4 behind.

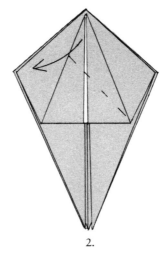

6. Repeat behind.

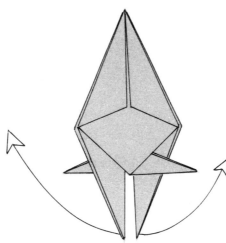

7. Pull out carefully.

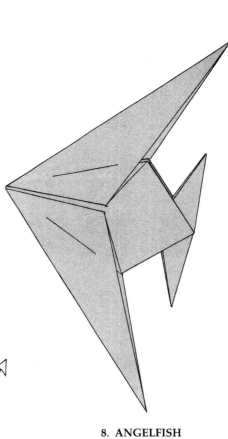

8. ANGELFISH

Starfish

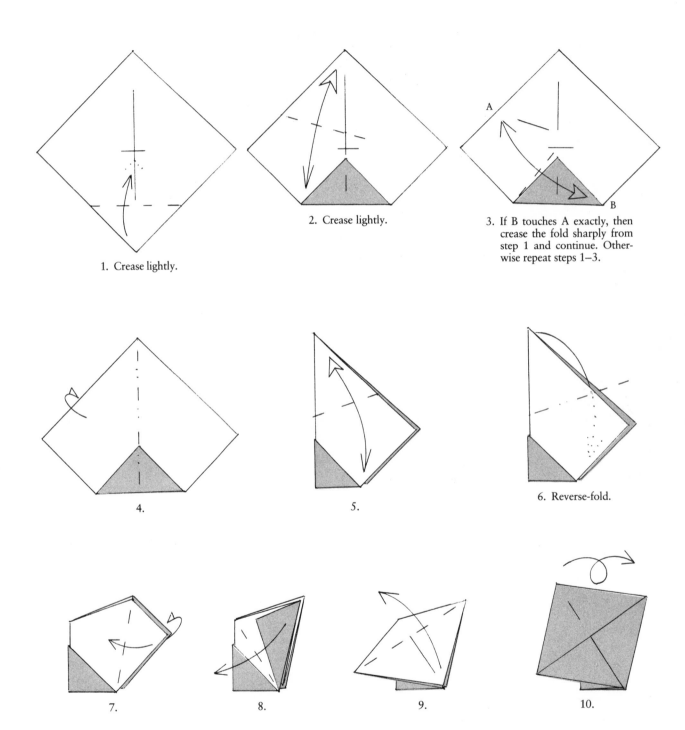

1. Crease lightly.

2. Crease lightly.

3. If B touches A exactly, then crease the fold sharply from step 1 and continue. Otherwise repeat steps 1–3.

4.

5.

6. Reverse-fold.

7.

8.

9.

10.

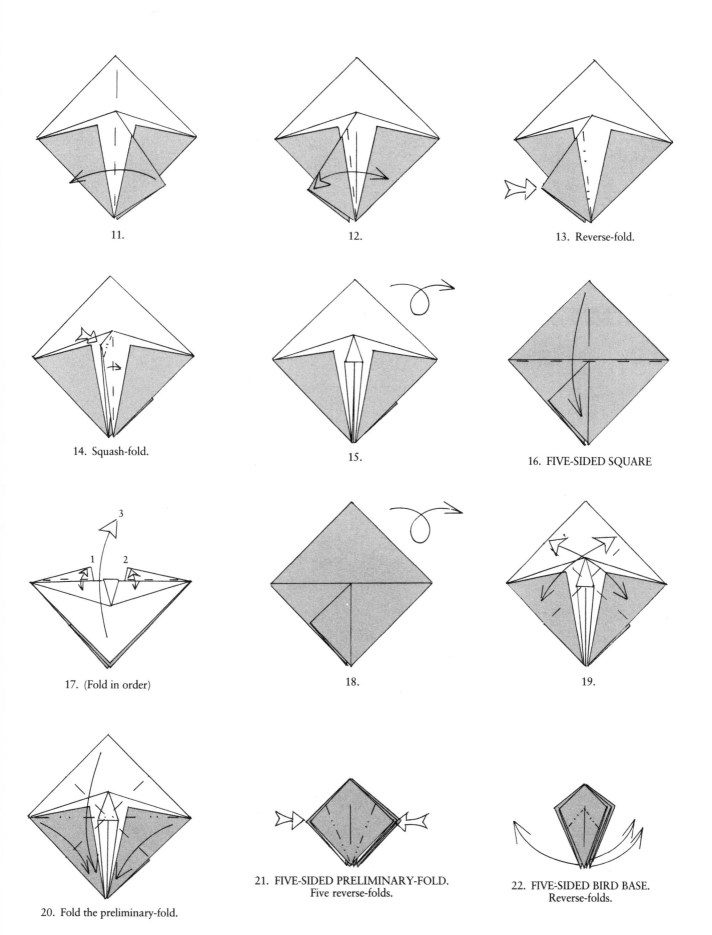

11.

12.

13. Reverse-fold.

14. Squash-fold.

15.

16. FIVE-SIDED SQUARE

17. (Fold in order)

18.

19.

20. Fold the preliminary-fold.

21. FIVE-SIDED PRELIMINARY-FOLD.
Five reverse-folds.

22. FIVE-SIDED BIRD BASE.
Reverse-folds.

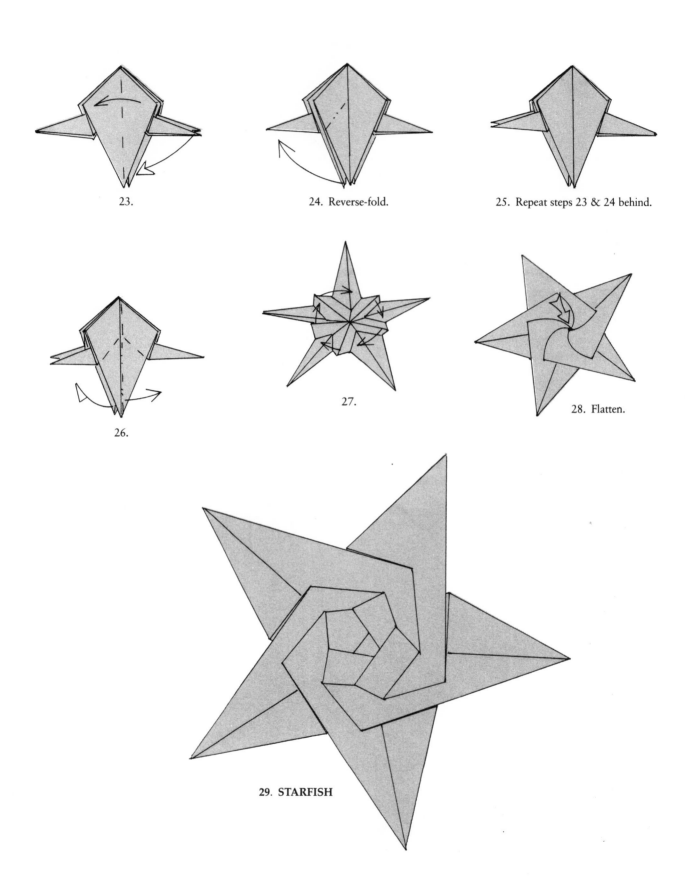

23.

24. Reverse-fold.

25. Repeat steps 23 & 24 behind.

26.

27.

28. Flatten.

29. STARFISH

Seal

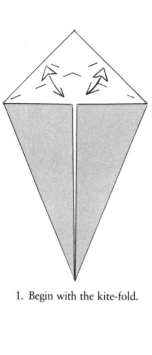

1. Begin with the kite-fold.

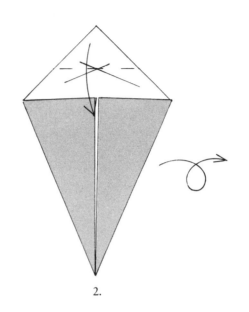

2.

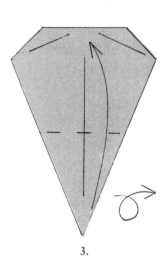

3.

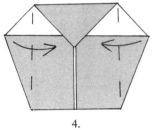

4.

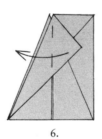

5.

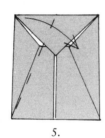

6.

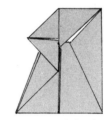

7. Repeat steps 5 & 6 on the right side.

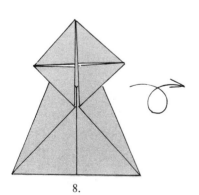

8.

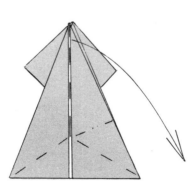

9. Rabbit ear.

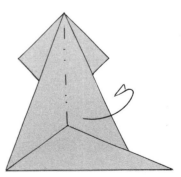

10.

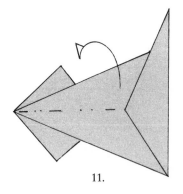

11.

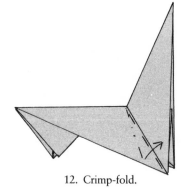

12. Crimp-fold.

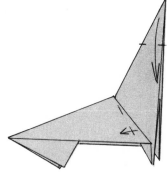

13. Repeat behind.

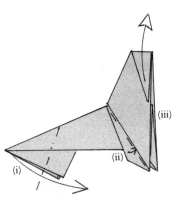

14. (i) Reverse-fold.
(ii) Tuck inside; repeat behind.
(iii) Unfold.

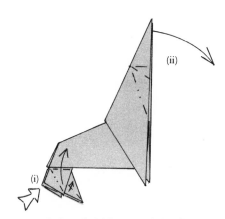

15. (i) Squash-fold; repeat behind.
(ii) Crimp-fold.

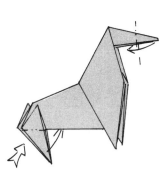

16. Reverse-fold inside the body.

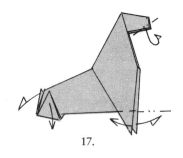

17.

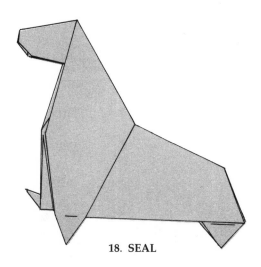

18. SEAL

Walrus

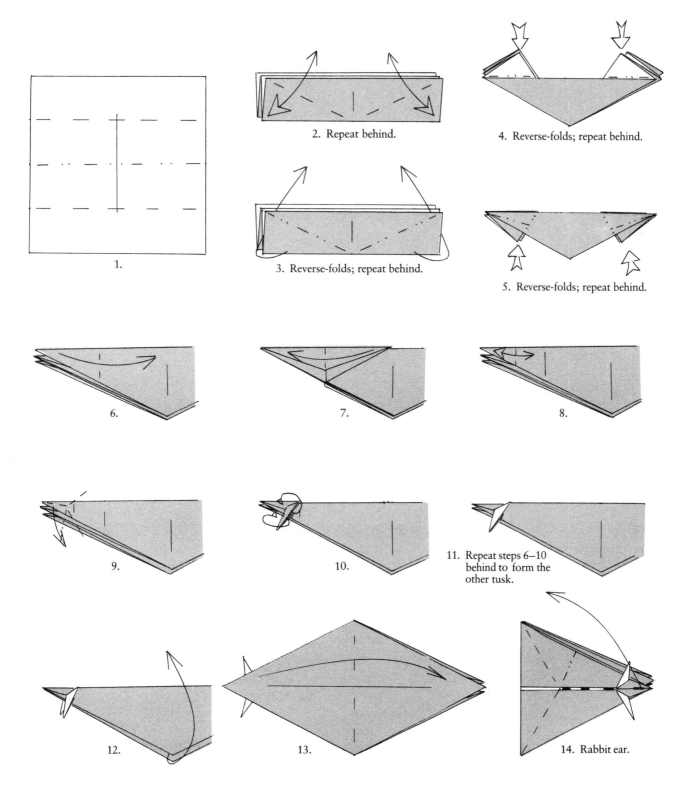

1.

2. Repeat behind.

3. Reverse-folds; repeat behind.

4. Reverse-folds; repeat behind.

5. Reverse-folds; repeat behind.

6.

7.

8.

9.

10.

11. Repeat steps 6–10 behind to form the other tusk.

12.

13.

14. Rabbit ear.

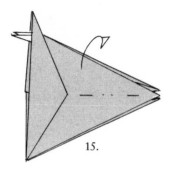

15.

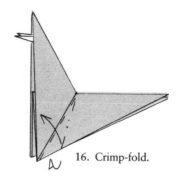

16. Crimp-fold.

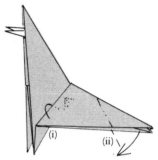

17. (i) Tuck inside.
(ii) Reverse-fold; repeat behind.

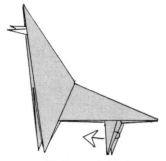

18. Repeat behind.

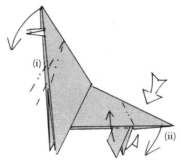

19. (i) Crimp-fold.
(ii) Reverse-fold.

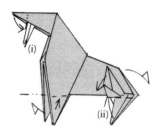

20. (i) Curve tusks.
(ii) Tuck inside.

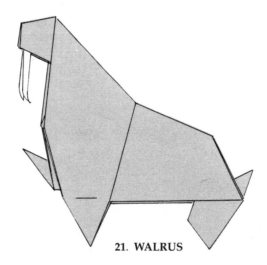

21. **WALRUS**

Sea Horse

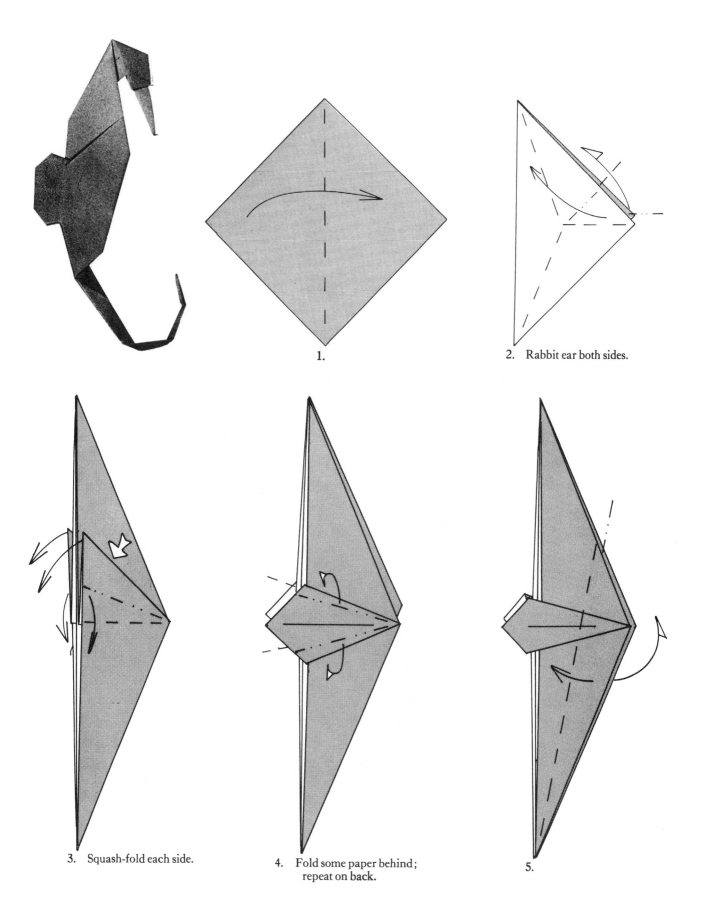

1.

2. Rabbit ear both sides.

3. Squash-fold each side.

4. Fold some paper behind; repeat on back.

5.

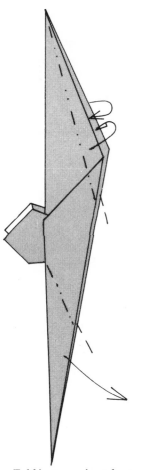

6. Fold in approximately one third of side. Inside reverse-fold to form tail.

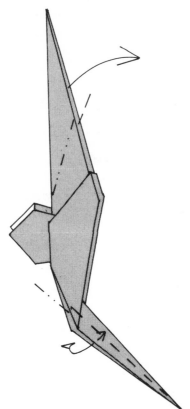

7. Inside reverse-fold to form head. Fold outside half of tail; repeat behind.

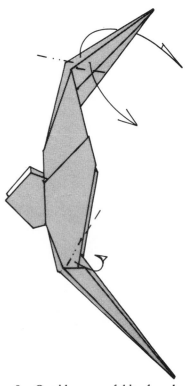

8. Outside reverse-fold to form head. Fold base of tail inside.

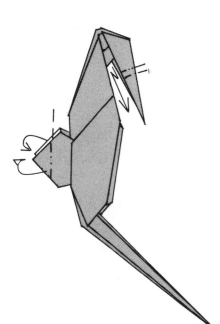

9. Inside crimp-fold. Fold tips of fin inside.

10. Reverse-fold tip inside nose. Curl tail with series of reverse-folds.

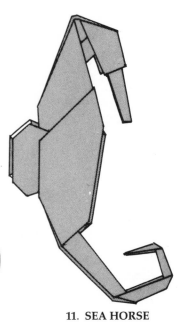

11. **SEA HORSE**

Whale

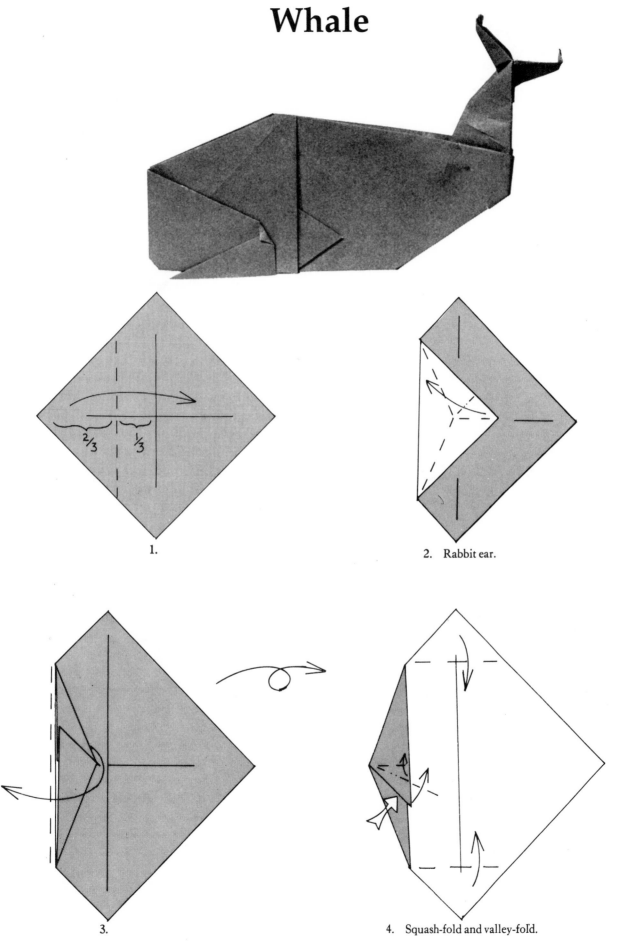

1.

2.   Rabbit ear.

3.

4.   Squash-fold and valley-fold.

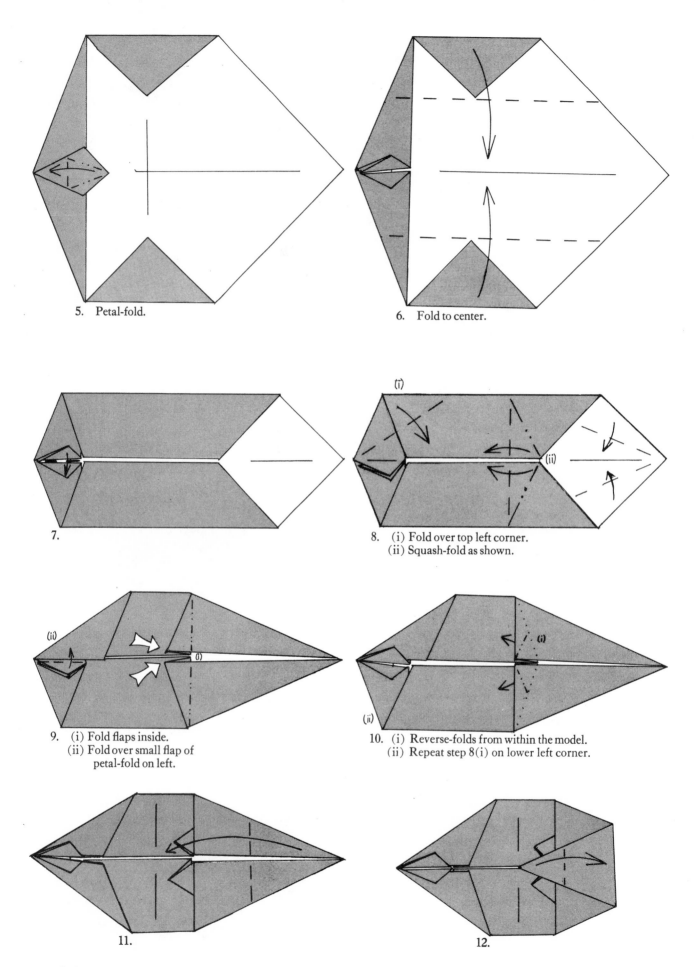

5. Petal-fold.

6. Fold to center.

7.

8. (i) Fold over top left corner.
   (ii) Squash-fold as shown.

9. (i) Fold flaps inside.
   (ii) Fold over small flap of
        petal-fold on left.

10. (i) Reverse-folds from within the model.
    (ii) Repeat step 8(i) on lower left corner.

11.

12.

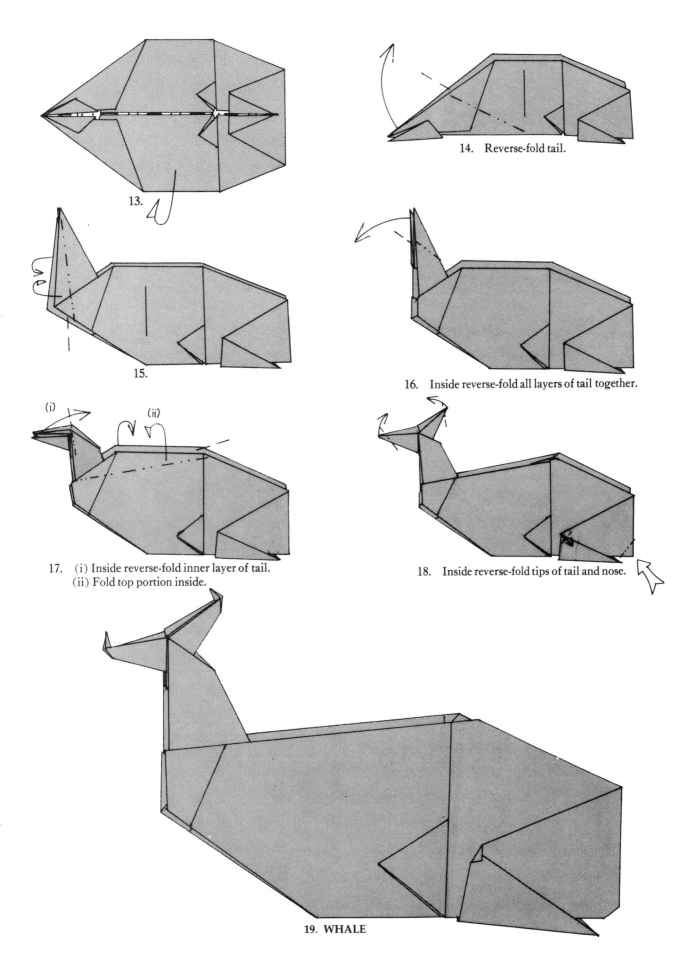

13.

14.   Reverse-fold tail.

15.

16.   Inside reverse-fold all layers of tail together.

17.   (i) Inside reverse-fold inner layer of tail.
      (ii) Fold top portion inside.

18.   Inside reverse-fold tips of tail and nose.

19. WHALE

Turtle

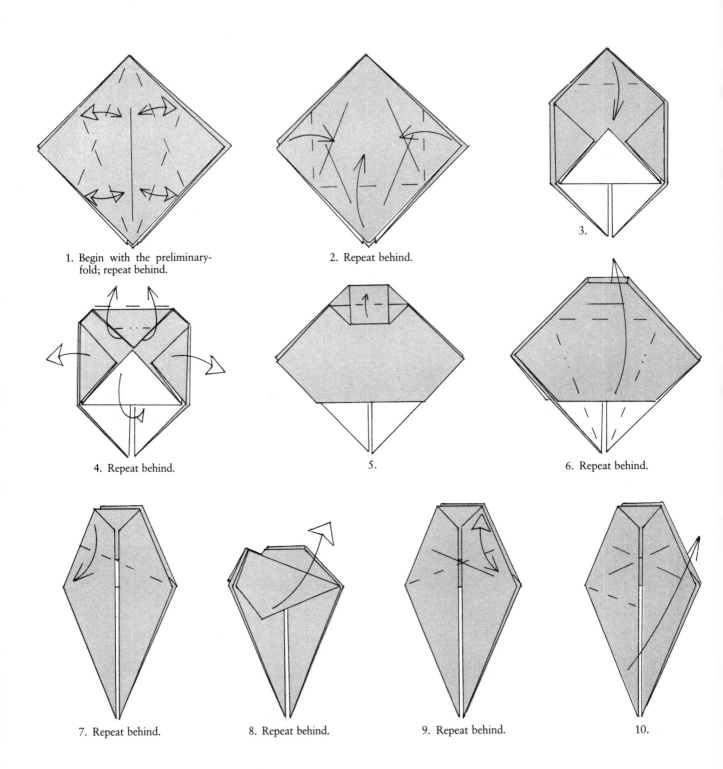

1. Begin with the preliminary-fold; repeat behind.

2. Repeat behind.

3.

4. Repeat behind.

5.

6. Repeat behind.

7. Repeat behind.

8. Repeat behind.

9. Repeat behind.

10.

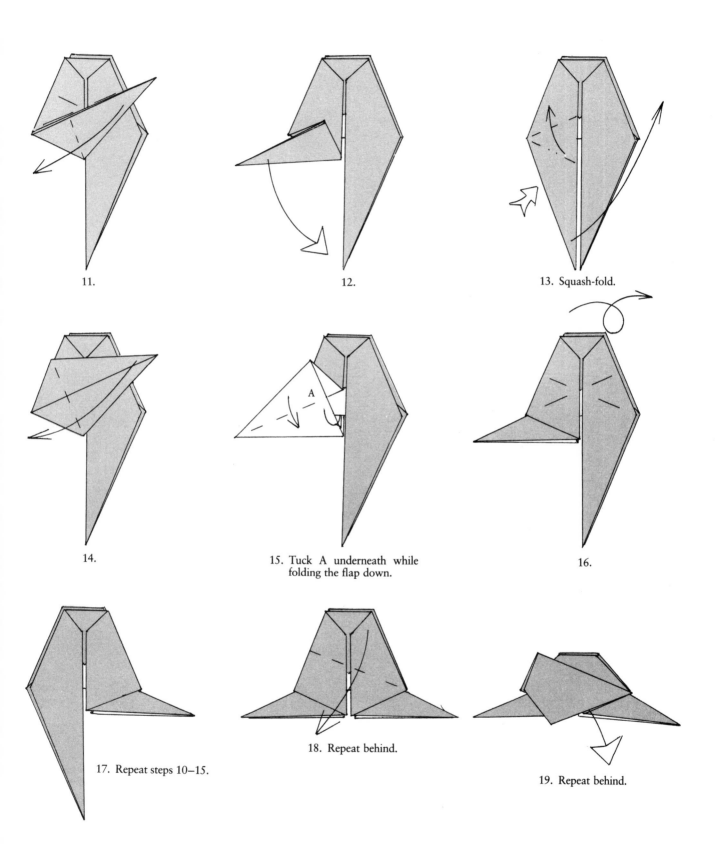

11.

12.

13. Squash-fold.

14.

15. Tuck A underneath while folding the flap down.

16.

17. Repeat steps 10–15.

18. Repeat behind.

19. Repeat behind.

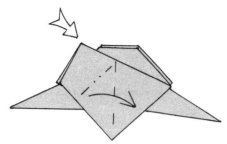

20. Repeat behind.

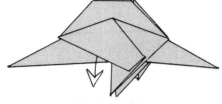

21. Repeat behind.

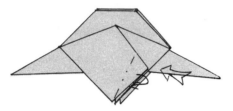

22. Repeat behind.

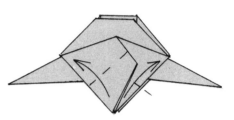

23. Repeat behind.

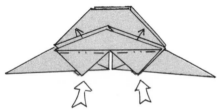

24. Reverse-folds; repeat behind.

25. Repeat behind.

26. Repeat behind.

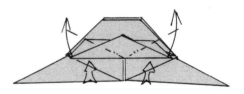

27. Reverse-folds; repeat behind.

28. Repeat behind.

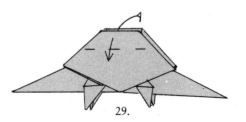

29.

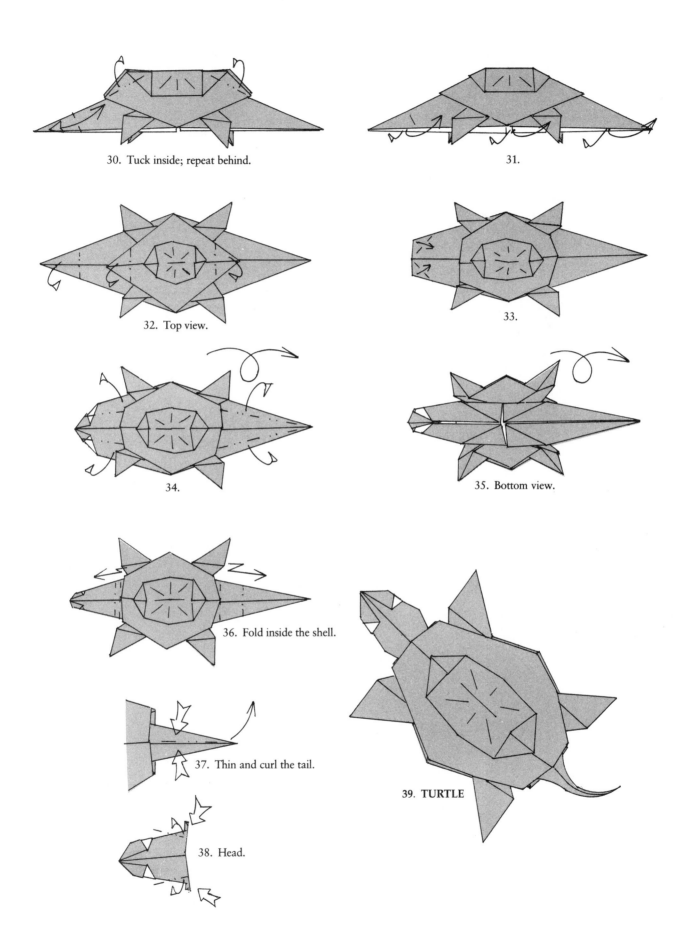

30. Tuck inside; repeat behind.

31.

32. Top view.

33.

34.

35. Bottom view.

36. Fold inside the shell.

37. Thin and curl the tail.

38. Head.

39. **TURTLE**

Frog

 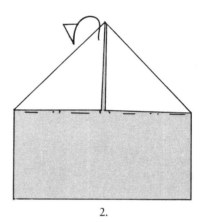

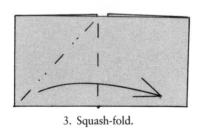 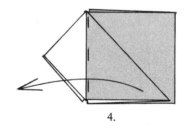

1.

2.

3. Squash-fold.

4.

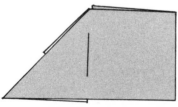 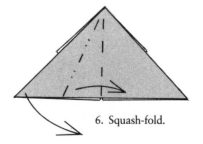

5. Repeat steps 3 & 4 on the right side.

6. Squash-fold.

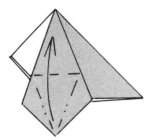

7. Petal-fold.

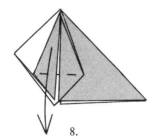

8.

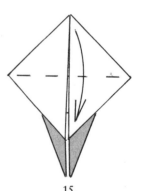

9.

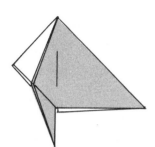

10. Repeat steps 6–9 on the right side.

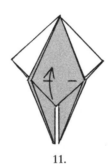

11.

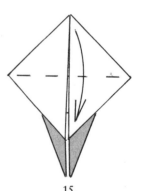

12.

13. Petal-fold.

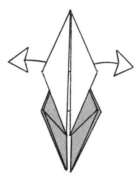

14. Pull out paper from inside.

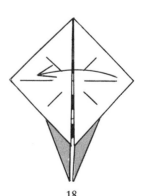

15.

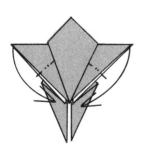

16. Reverse-folds.

17.

18.

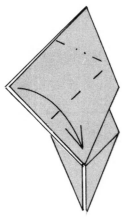

19. Squash-fold.

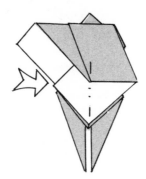

20. Reverse-fold.

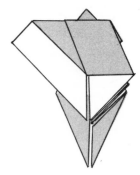

21. Unfold to step 18.

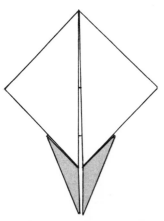

22. Repeat steps 18–21 on the left and, using these new creases, fold them together to form step 23.

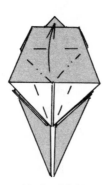

23. Petal-fold.

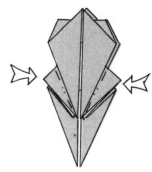

24. Reverse-folds.

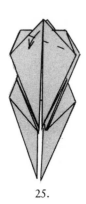

25.

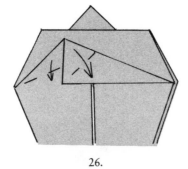

26.

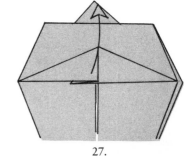

27.

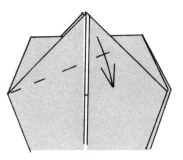

28.

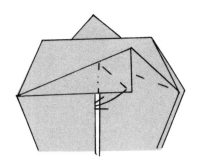

29. Tuck inside.

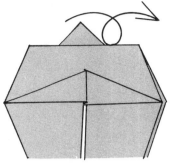

30.

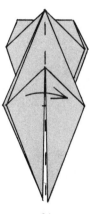

31.

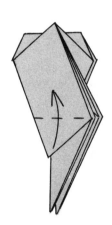

32.

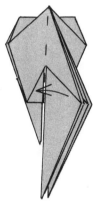

33.

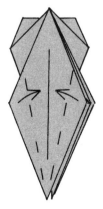

34.

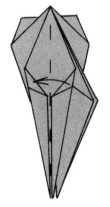

35. Repeat steps 31–35 on the right side.

36.

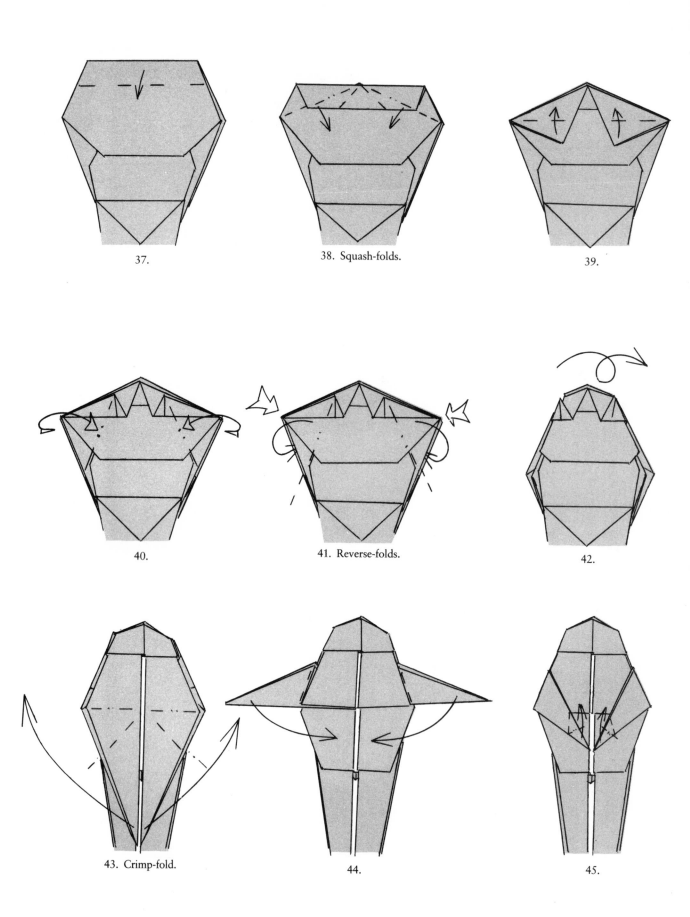

37.

38. Squash-folds.

39.

40.

41. Reverse-folds.

42.

43. Crimp-fold.

44.

45.

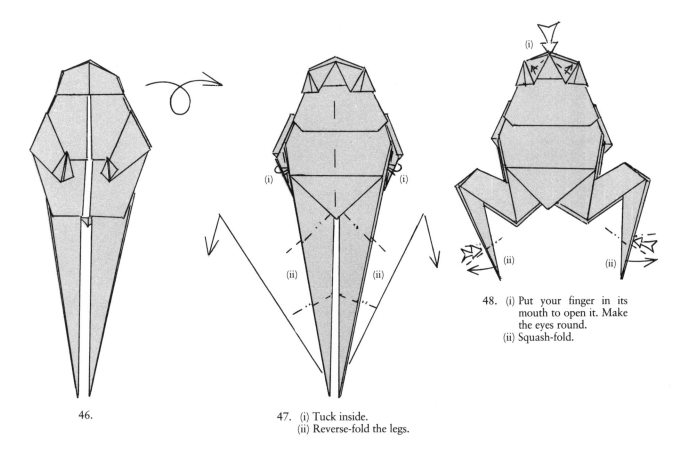

46.

47. (i) Tuck inside.
(ii) Reverse-fold the legs.

48. (i) Put your finger in its mouth to open it. Make the eyes round.
(ii) Squash-fold.

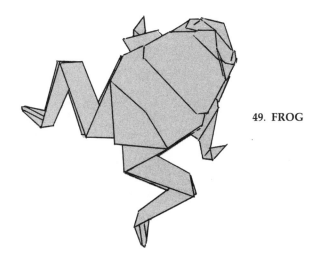

49. FROG

Crab

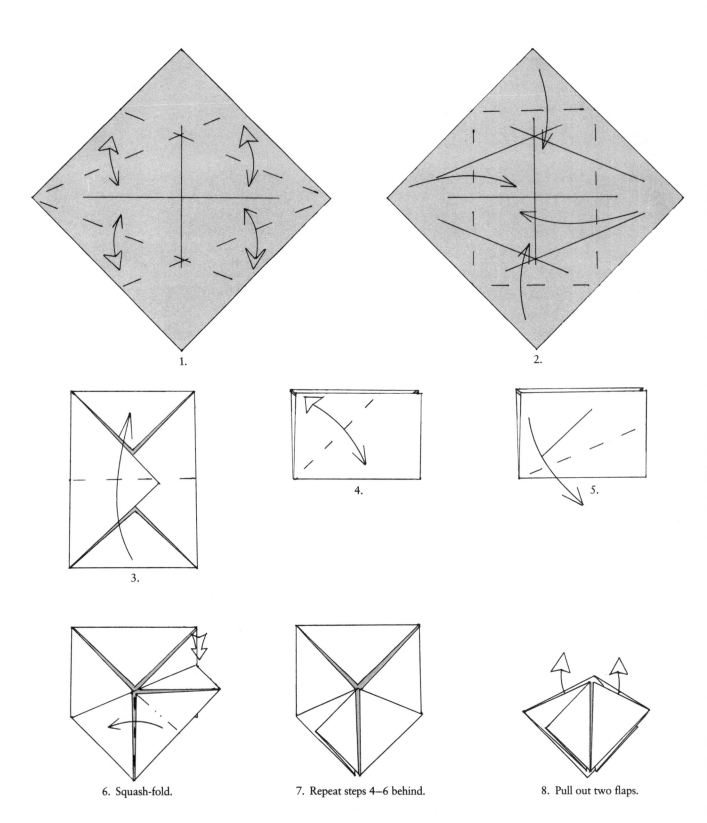

1.

2.

3.

4.

5.

6. Squash-fold.

7. Repeat steps 4–6 behind.

8. Pull out two flaps.

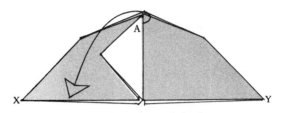

9.

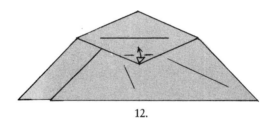

10. (Do not repeat behind)

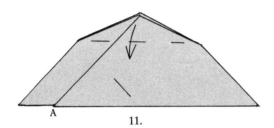

11.

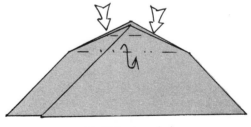

12.

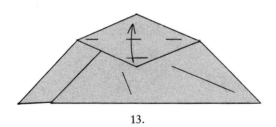

13.

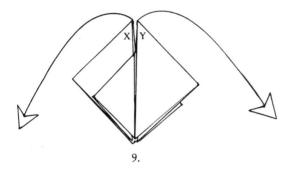

14. Sink triangularly.

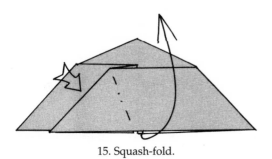

15. Squash-fold.

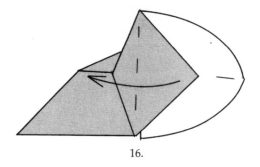

16.

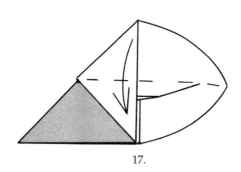

17.

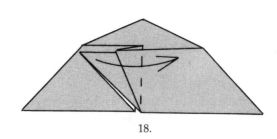

18.

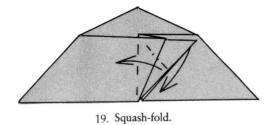

19. Squash-fold.

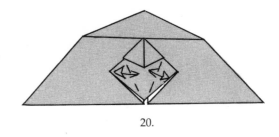

20.

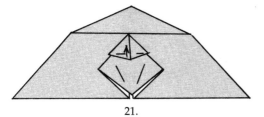

21.

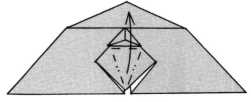

22. Petal-fold.

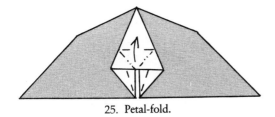

23.

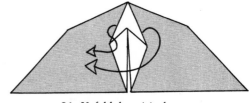

24. Squash-fold.

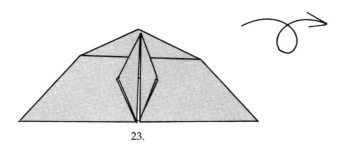

25. Petal-fold.

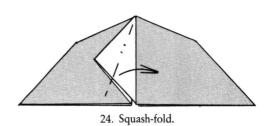

26. Unfold the original corner.

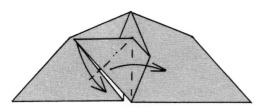

27. Squash-fold.

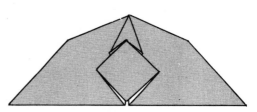

28. Fold half of the brontosaurus base.

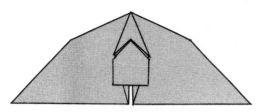

29. Fold the small triangle underneath.

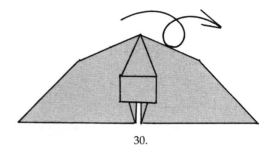

30.

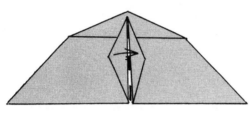

31.

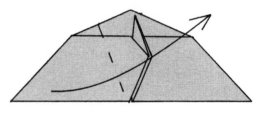

32.

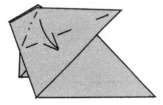

33. Squash-fold.

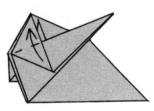

34.

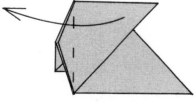

35.

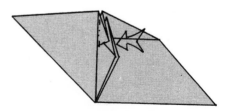

36. Reverse-fold.

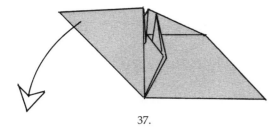

37.

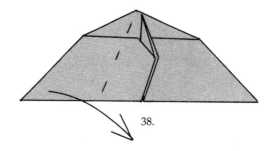

38.

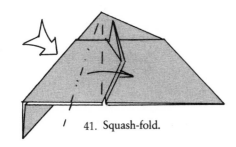

39.

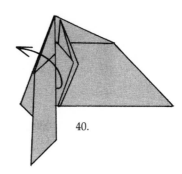

40.

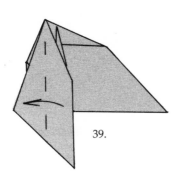

41. Squash-fold.

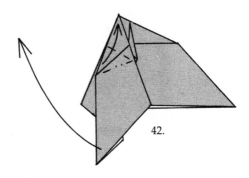

42.

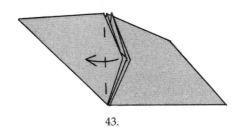

43.

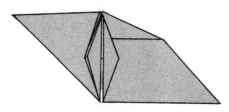

44. Repeat steps 32-43 on the right side.

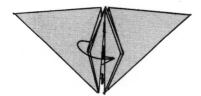

45. Repeat behind.

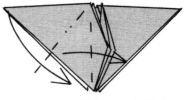

46. Squash-fold; repeat behind.

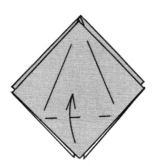

47. Repeat behind.

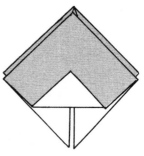

48. Wing-fold.

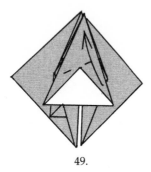

49.

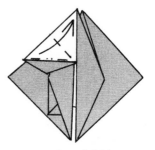

50. Squash-fold.

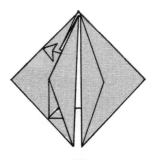

51. Reverse-fold.

52.

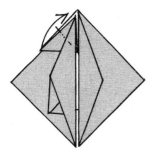

53. Reverse-fold.

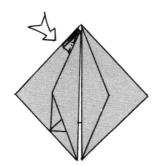

54. Reverse-folds.

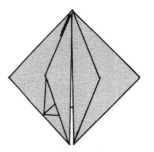

55. Repeat steps 48-54 behind.

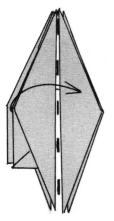

56. Repeat behind.

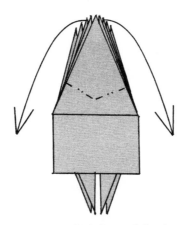

57. Reverse-fold three of the four flaps together on each side.

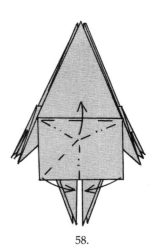

58.

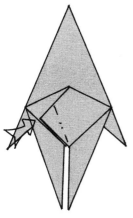

59. Reverse-fold.

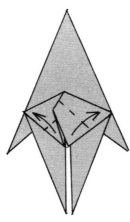

60.

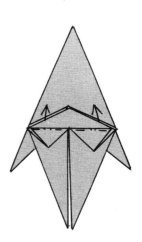

61. Reverse-folds.

Crab 45

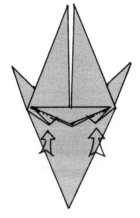

62. (Model rotated) Reverse-folds.

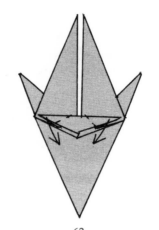

63.

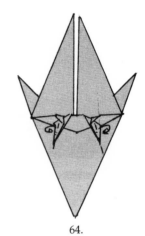

64.

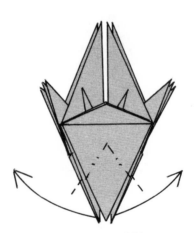

65.

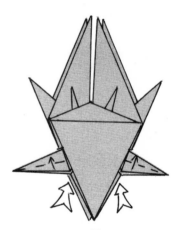

66. Reverse-folds.

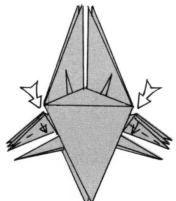

67.

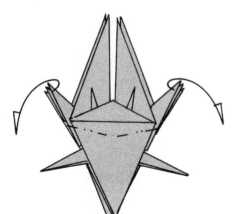

68. Mountain-fold all the layers together.

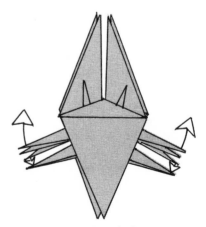

69.

70. Separate the legs.

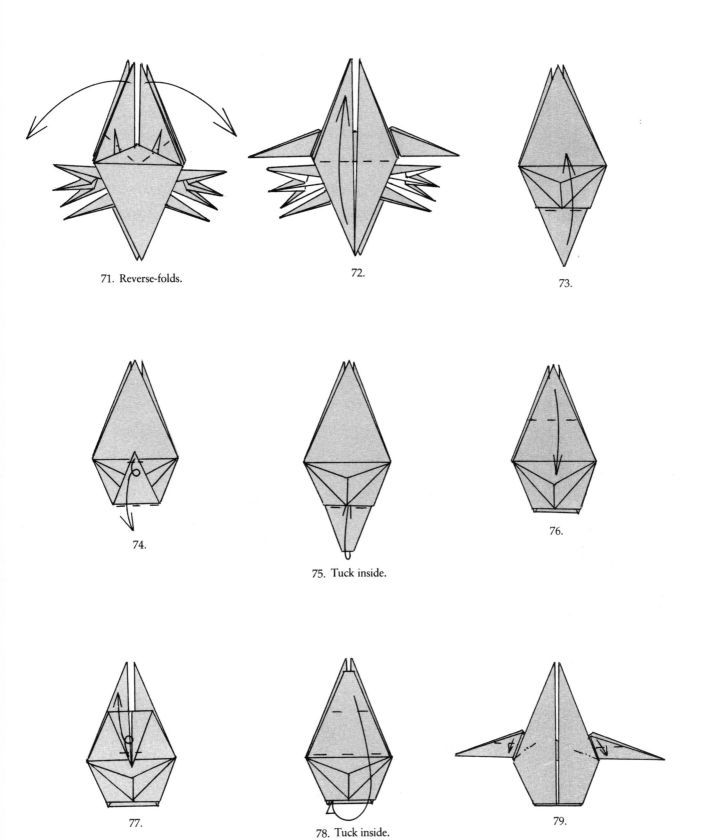

71. Reverse-folds.

72.

73.

74.

75. Tuck inside.

76.

77.

78. Tuck inside.

79.

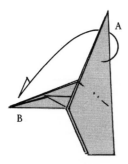

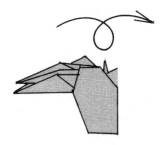

80. Mountain-fold flap A into flap B; repeat on the right.

81. Repeat on the right.

82.

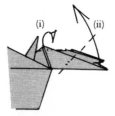

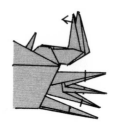

83. (i) Tuck inside.
    (ii) Reverse-fold the pinchers together; repeat on the left side.

84. Open the claw; repeat on the left side.

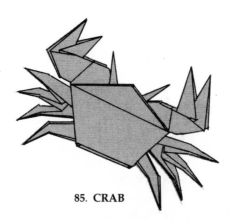

85. CRAB